The Rainbow
Writing the Research Paper

Karen Blomain
Mary Keenan Hart
Susan R. Ide
Charlotte Ravaioli

Keystone Junior College

Kendall/Hunt
Publishing Company
Dubuque, Iowa

This edition has been printed directly from camera ready copy.

Copyright © 1987 by Kendall/Hunt Publishing Company

ISBN 0-8403-4557-7

Printed in the United States of America
10   9   8   7   6   5   4   3   2

TABLE OF CONTENTS

ACKNOWLEDGMENTS

We owe a special thanks

to our students, whose ideas, experiences and hard work helped us to develop this text, and especially to Marc Tobin, who designed the Workbook cover;

to our colleagues, who provided us with suggestions, feedback and encouragement;

to Keystone Junior College and its Faculty Development Committee, whose support allowed us to pull this all together.

Dear Writer,

When you hear the words "Research Paper," do your hands shake, does your throat tighten, and does your stomach become a hard knot? We know the feeling! Each of us has written dozens of research papers and assigned research papers to hundreds of students. We know how swamped such a big and complex project can make a writer feel. That´s why we´ve spent years developing a process for doing research papers that takes out most of the pain and guarantees success.

This Workbook takes you through the process step by step. By focusing on one step at a time, you won´t feel overwhelmed, but will experience satisfaction as you complete each step. When the paper is assigned, ask your instructor to give you due dates for each step so that you can easily budget your time. Write the due date for each step in the spaces provided in the Workbook.

Before you begin, we recommend that you assemble the materials you´ll need to complete the project: 3" x 5" and/or 4" x 6" cards, a comfortable pen, paper clips, rubber bands, lined notebook paper or legal pad paper, and a manila envelope at least 10" x 13". We suggest that you keep in the manila envelope all the material for each step as you complete it.

Before you get to the notetaking step, please take a few minutes to color-code the sample research at the end of the Workbook. You will need crayons, markers, or pencils in nine colors. Use a different color to underline or highlight each of the sources listed in the bibliography. Then in the text of the paper underline or highlight information from each source with the same color you used for that source in the bibliography. For example, you might use yellow for the source by Ellen Bassuk and for all the information in the paper taken from the Bassuk source. Color-coding the sample research paper will help you to see how note cards work in the paper, how you can integrate source material in the paper, and how your own comments (the remaining white spaces) make your paper truly your own.

The rainbow is a symbol of achievement and good fortune. We know that The Rainbow process will lead you to success in your research paper.

Sincerely,

Karen, Mary, Susan
and Charlotte

1

STEP 1:   TOPIC SEARCH AND SELECTION   Due date:____

     On this page, list things you are interested in, even if you don´t know much about them.

Things of interest to me

1. _____   11. _____

2. _____   12. _____

3. _____   13. _____

4. _____   14. _____

5. _____   15. _____

6. _____   16. _____

7. _____   17. _____

8. _____   18. _____

9. _____   19. _____

10. _____   20. _____

Examine your list. Find one or two topics that draw your attention right now. Write them in the spaces provided. Break each down into smaller units, if possible. List the smaller units under each of the two topics.

TOPIC A: *CARS*   TOPIC B: *Dreams*

1. FAST   1. _____
2. SLOW   2. _____
3. ECONOMY   3. _____
4. ULGY   4. _____
5. EXPENSIVE   5. _____
6. CHEAP   6. _____
7. FORDS   7. _____
8. CHEVYS   8. _____
9. FORD VS. CHEVY   9. _____
*10. RACING   10. _____

Decide which topic you would enjoy working with. Write it here:

Racing cars. Dreams

Is the topic current?
Does the topic seem too broad?
Does the topic seem too narrow?
Can I take a stand on the topic?

Instructor's OK: Completion date:____

3

STEP 2: PREWRITING   Due date:____

1.   Write down everything you know about your research paper
topic in the Prewriting column. Include opinions, personal
experiences, beliefs, and facts.

2.   After you have written down all that you know about your
research paper topic, write down all the questions that you
have about it in the Questions column.

3.   Now have someone else read all that you have written so
far. Ask your reader to write all that he or she knows about
your research paper topic, and then to add questions about it
that he or she would like to have answered. If you have
time, ask several people to read the prewriting and to write
down their knowledge and questions. Use as many additional
sheets of paper as you need.

Instructor´s OK: Completion date:____

Topic: _____

Prewriting   Questions
_____   _____

Prewriting | Questions

STEP 3: ORGANIZING PREWRITING QUESTIONS   Due date:____

Read over your sheet(s) of questions from Step 2. Write the first question in box #1. If the second question is closely related to the first, write that in box #1 also. If not, write it in box #2. Continue writing questions, grouping related ones in appropriate boxes. When you have finished, write a label for each box in the space provided.

Instructor's OK: Completion date:_____

#1 LABEL	#2 LABEL

#3   LABEL

#4   LABEL

#5   LABEL

#6   LABEL

STEP 4:   READERS´ GUIDE   Refer to the sample page of
                                      Readers´ Guide

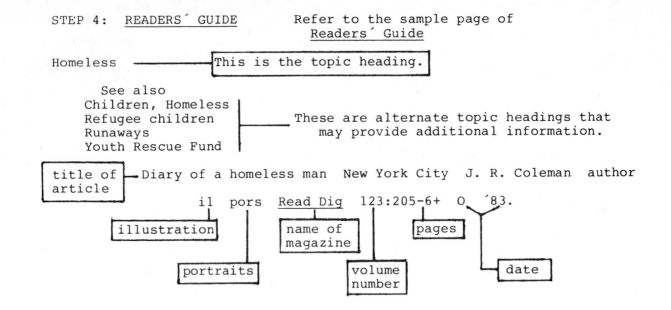

READERS´GUIDE QUESTIONNAIRE

1.   Find an article on Winslow Homer that includes a bibliography.

2.   What article on homemakers appeared in July 1983?

3.   What heading would you use to find Home storage?

4.   In what magazine does D. Peerman´s article on homeless people appear?

5.   Which magazine provides most of the information on homesteads?

6.   What magazine and page numbers contain an article by Carolyn L.
     Hommel?

7.   What other headings would you check for the topic "Homeless"?

8.   Find one entry under any heading on this page that has both an
     illustration and a portrait.

9.   Who are the co-authors of an article on homeostasis?

10. What is the date of the New York magazine article entitled "AIDS
     Anxiety"?

STEP 5A: BIBLIOGRAPHY SEARCH   Due date:____

SAMPLE BIB FORMAT

Author's last name(,) First name(.) (")Title

of Article(.)(") Name of Magazine day month

year(:) page numbers(.)

You will need 25 lined 3 x 5 cards for your bib search.
A completed card is shown here and an example emphasizing
correct punctuation appears above. When your 25 bib cards
are done, secure them with a rubber band. It's a good idea
at this point to buy a large manila envelope to keep bib
cards and other materials together.

SAMPLE BIB CARD

Andersen, K. "Left Out in the Cold."

Time 19 December 1983: 14-15.

Instructor's OK: Completion date:____

STEP 5B: SEARCH FOR SOURCES

On this sheet, keep a record of the indexes you have checked, the topic headings you have looked under in each source, and how many articles you found.

POSSIBLE INDEXES:

Readers´ Guide   New York Times Index
Social Sciences Index   Education Index
National Geographic Index   NewsBank
Pamphlet File   Card Catalogue
Social Issues Resource Series (SIRS)
Other _____

Index	Volume number and date	Heading	Number of articles

STEP 6:   EVALUATING AND SELECTING SOURCES   Due date:____

As you skim through your sources, ask the following questions to determine if each will be useful for your paper.

1. Can I understand the language of the article?

2. Is the article long enough to provide useful information?

3. Does this article seem to answer the questions I've raised?

4. Is this material repetitious?

5. Is the information current?

6. Does this article seem fair?

7. Does this article contain factual information about my topic or is it just one person's story?

With these questions in mind, select and photocopy your best articles--at least seven of them. DO NOT TEAR PAGES FROM THE LIBRARY'S MAGAZINES OR NEWSPAPERS. Make sure that the following appear somewhere on the first page of each article: author's name, title of article, name of magazine and date. Be sure that a page number appears on each page of the article.   Missing information should be handwritten on the photocopy. If an article has more than one page, staple the pages together.

Instructor's OK: Completion date:____

Process Notes

Write about your research experience so far. What have
you learned? What problems have you run into? What was
easy? Why? What was frustrating? Why? What would you do
differently next time?

Step 7A: NOTE CARDS AND NOTETAKING

A note card should be written in ink on one side of a 3 x 5 or 4 x 6 card. It should include the following five parts:

1. the last name of the
    author or authors

> a. If there is no author cited, either at the beginning or the end of the article, use the title of the article in quotation marks.
>
> b. If you have two articles by the same author, you'll have to include the title of the article along with the author's name.

2. the page on which the
    information appears

> If you turn the page of your article as you record the author's words or ideas, you must indicate that page turn with a slash (/) and record the new page number.

3. the information you
    want to record

> ONLY ONE IDEA should be written on a card.

4. a label for the
   type of note you have
   taken

   a) direct quote
   b) paraphrase
   c) summary
   d) combination of any of the
      first three
   e) personal comment

5. a slug

   a word or phrase that specifically
   reflects the information you have
   written on the card.

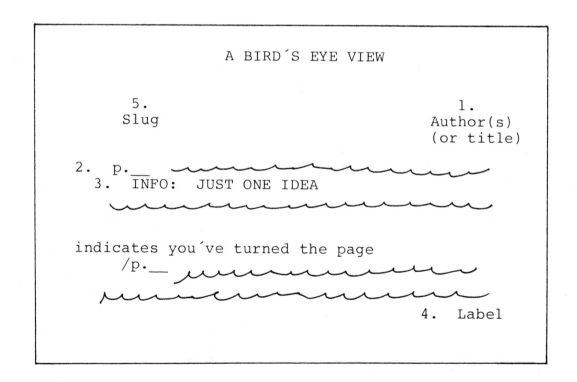

NOTETAKING

First, read through your article and make marginal notations or underline sections that provide answers to the questions you have already asked about your topic. Now you are ready to record the information you have found, but you need to decide how you will _word_ that information when you write it on your card. There are four different ways to record information or ideas _someone else_ has written about. You may write 1) a direct quote, 2) a paraphrase, 3) a summary, or 4) a combination of 1, 2, or 3.

DIRECT QUOTE

A direct quote means you copy the information onto your card _EXACTLY_ (identical wording, spelling, capitalization, and punctuation) as it appears in the article you are reading. Quotation marks are needed--at the beginning and end of what you have copied. A direct quote is _not_ just something which is already written within quotation marks in the article. (All note samples in this section are from Steven Fustero's article, "Home on the Street," which appeared in the February 1984 issue of _Psychology Today_.)

Solutions-negative   Fustero

p. 60   "Phoenix has been especially inventive in its
dealings with the homeless. In 1982, the city decided
to rid itself of the homeless population because it
felt these people were scaring away tourists and
potentially lucrative business prospects."

Direct   quote

VARIATIONS

1.   Sometimes you may be quoting a long passage and
discover that you don´t need all the words or sentences to
convey the meaning. You may leave out some of the author´s
words, but you must replace them with ellipsis, three spaced
dots (. . .). Here is the original:

>   The merchants of Bethesda have expressed several
>
>   concerns in their series of meetings with the
>
>   county. Foremost on their list is the fear that
>
>   the kitchen, along with its group of indigent men,
>
>   will disrupt business during the day and create a
>
>   safety problem at night. (Fustero 60)

Here´s how ellipsis can be used:

```
 _____
|                                                           |
| Problems they cause-businesses               Fustero      |
|                                                           |
|    p. 60  "The merchants of Bethesda have expressed       |
| several  concerns. . . . Foremost . . . is the fear       |
| that the kitchen . . . will disrupt business during       |
| the day and create a safety problem at night."            |
|                                                           |
|                               Direct quote                |
|_____|
```

2.   If a word or section of your direct quote needs
clarification, or you want to summarize a section that you´ve
left out of the quote, you may use brackets and insert an
explanation.

```
┌─────────────────────────────────────────────────────────┐
│ Solutions-negative                          Fustero      │
│                                                          │
│  p. 60  "In 1982, the city [Phoenix, Arizona]            │
│ decided to rid itself of the homeless population         │
│ because it felt these people were scaring away           │
│ tourists."                                               │
│                                                          │
│                                          Direct quote    │
└─────────────────────────────────────────────────────────┘
```

WHEN SHOULD YOU USE A DIRECT QUOTE?

Research papers which depend on too many direct quotes or a number of lengthy direct quotes will make your reader wonder whether or not you really understand your topic. In addition, too many direct quotes will drown out your voice and cause your reader to wonder if you are really the author of the paper. To avoid what is often called a "cut and paste" job (you have cut certain sentences or sections out of many articles and have just pasted them into your paper), choose your direct quotes carefully. A few rules of thumb may help you.

A direct quote should be used only if:

a) you are convinced that the information you want to record is worded so well that you'd lose the clarity or tone of the original if you changed the wording;

b) the author is defining or describing something complicated and you're afraid you may misinterpret his idea;

c) the author is an authority on the subject and his words will support his or your opinion.

If none of these conditions exists, you should either paraphrase or summarize the information.

PARAPHRASE

To paraphrase means to put the author's information or opinion into your own words. A note which is paraphrased is about the same length as the original. Sometimes writers think that paraphrasing means substituting synonynms for the author's words--or shifting the words around in the sentence. Neither will lead to an accurately written paraphrase. Read the following quotation. (All note samples which follow will be based on this quotation.)

> Phoenix has been especially inventive in its
> dealings with the homeless. In 1982, the city
> decided to rid itself of the homeless population
> because it felt these people were scaring away
> tourists and potentially lucrative business
> prospects. So, Phoenix began a dispersal
> policy. (Fustero 60)

Now read an inaccurately paraphrased note which is based on the preceding quote.

Solutions-negative   Fustero

    p. 60 Phoenix has been very creative in dealing
with its street people and vagrants. Because the
city fathers believed that these people were scaring
away tourists and potentially lucrative business
prospects, in 1982, the city decided to rid itself
of the homeless population. Thus the city instituted
its dispersal policy.

Paraphrase

What's wrong with this note card? The student's first sentence is almost the same as the writer's except that she

19

has substituted synonyms for the words "inventive" and "homeless." The wording of her second sentence illustrates another mistake: she has just changed a few words and switched the parts of the sentence around. Neither sentence is written in her own words nor do the sentences reflect her own style of writing.

To ensure that what you write is really written in your own words and in your own style, you might try this. Carefully read the passage you want to use. Close the magazine. Now restate the information in your own words. Open the magazine and check that what you have written is in your own words and has captured the author's ideas or data. Here's an example of an accurately written paraphrase based on the Fustero passage.

Solutions-negative   Fustero

  p. 60 The city fathers in Phoenix, Arizona, were
alarmed by what they believed to be the damaging
effect that the homeless had on their tourist
image and their ability to attract new,
profitable businesses to the city. As a result
they developed policies which encouraged the
homeless to leave Phoenix as soon as they
arrived.

                                        Paraphrase

SUMMARY

A summary is also written in your own words and it involves your recording the author's key idea. The note you write on your card will be much shorter than the original.

An example follows:

Solutions-negative   Fustero

p. 60 In 1982 Phoenix enacted ordinances that forced the homeless to go elsewhere.

Summary

COMBINATION

This type of note does what its label says. It combines two forms of notetaking: 1) the direct quote and the summary or paraphrase or 2) the summary and the paraphrase. The first form of combination note is more common. It is useful when you can easily paraphrase or summarize some of the material but you would like to use a few effective phrases or sentences word for word. You must remember to enclose the material you are quoting within quotation marks.

Solutions-negative   Fustero

p. 60 In 1982, Phoenix, Arizona, decided that the homeless in the city were destroying the city´s tourist image and its "potentially lucrative business prospects." As a result the city fathers developed a "dispersal policy."

Paraphrase/direct quote

PERSONAL COMMENT

As you are recording information from your articles, you may want to make your own observations, or ask questions that you think haven´t been fully answered, or try to recognize and account for bits of information that appear to be contradictory. There are two ways you can do this:

1. Record your reaction directly on the note card where you have already written your direct quote, paraphrase, summary or combination note. In this case you will write your comment at the bottom of the note card and enclose it within brackets [ ].

2. Write your own personal comment on a separate note card. Set the card up like all other cards, create a slug, use your own initials to indicate that you are the author.

YOUR NEXT STEP

When you have completed taking notes on an article, arrange the note cards in the order in which they appear in the photocopy. Paper clip the cards to the article.

STEP 7B: PLAGIARISM

Plagiarism occurs when any writer borrows another author's words, facts, or ideas and fails to give credit to the author. In effect, the student who writes a paper and fails to give credit where credit is due, is saying "these words and ideas are mine and originated with me"--when the words and ideas are really the brainchild of someone else. Obviously this is dishonest. Often, however, plagiarism occurs unintentionally. A student may paraphrase inaccurately or forget to tell her reader that she has borrowed words or ideas. But, whether intentional or not, plagiarism in any form can have very serious academic consequences for a student.

In order to avoid plagiarism, you must make sure that you:

1. carefully follow the instructions for recording your notes;

2. paraphrase carefully;

3. use quotation marks to let your reader know when you are using a direct quote;

4. document the source of each note whenever you use a note card;

5. list all the sources you have used on your bibliography page.

Process Notes on Notetaking

STEP 8:   COMPLETION OF NOTETAKING   Due date:_____
           AND PEER REVIEW OF NOTE CARDS

        As you finish taking notes on each article, attach the
cards with a paper clip to the article they go with. Be sure
that the cards are in the same order as the information
appears in the article.

        Give this sheet, your note cards and photocopies to your
partner to review.

My name is _____. I am reading

_____ ´s note cards.

        Read   over   your partner´s note cards carefully to
determine if each meets the following requirements:

        1.   Slug line?

        2.   Author´s name?

        3.   Page number(s)?

        4.   Type of note card?

        5.   One idea per card?

        If any of these areas is missing or inaccurate, jot a
word or two to that effect on the back of the card.

Overall Impression:

        When you have read all of your partner´s note cards,
answer the following questions on this sheet.

In general:

        6.   Are the note cards legible?
        7.   Are there too many quotations?
        8.   Is there enough factual information?
        9.   Is there one idea per card?
       10.   Make any further comments on page 26.

        Return note cards and photocopies to your partner in
the same order that you got them along with this sheet.

Additional Reviewer Comments:

When you get your materials back, make any necessary corrections on the cards, and attach them again with the paper clip to the article they came from. Hand in corrected note cards, photocopies and this review sheet to your instructor.

Instructor´s OK: Completion date:_____

STEP 9:   FORMULATING A THESIS STATEMENT   Due date:_____

    If I were to ask you what your paper is about at this point, you would say that it's about_____.

    Then I might ask, "Well, what <u>about</u> it? What's your opinion about your topic now that you've spent so much time thinking, reading and writing about it?"

    And you would say, "After thinking, reading and writing about it all this time, I think the bottom line is that

_____."

    It is possible that what you've written above is your thesis statement, the main point of all your reading, thinking and writing. Look at what you've written in the last few blanks. Check to see if it has these parts:

1.   Is your TOPIC stated clearly?

        Example: homeless in America

2.   Is your OPINION about your TOPIC stated clearly?

        Example: It's society's responsibility to provide them with food, clothing, shelter and medical care.

3.   If your thesis deals with a problem, is there a METHOD OR SOLUTION advocated?

        Example: Federal, state and local government tax money, as well as private funding, should be earmarked for their care.

4.   Does your opinion pertain to your WHOLE TOPIC and not just to one segment of it?

        Example: NOT   Phoenix should change its laws.

5.   Is your opinion DIRECTLY RELATED to the reading and thinking you've done?

        If you can answer yes to the questions above, you probably have a good thesis statement. Write it out here.

_____

Instructor's OK: Completion date:_____

STEP 10:   WRITING AN INTRODUCTION   Due date:_____
           FOR THE RESEARCH PAPER

     Try writing three different introductions to your paper
by using three of the suggestions below or others that you
think of.   Look again at your prewriting for ideas. Your
goal is to grab your reader´s attention at the same time that
you let her know what your thesis is.

   1.   Explain how you got interested in your topic in the
        first place.

   2.   Mention surpising statistics and/or other facts about
        your topic.

   3.   Narrate a brief story related to your topic.

   4.   Describe a personal experience related to your topic.

   5.   Tell what is controversial about your topic.

   6.   Tell what most people believe about your topic,
        especially if later on in your paper you plan to
        present factual information that shows most people
        are misguided.

   7.   Explain your opinion about the topic and tell how your
        opinion changed from the time you began working on the
        paper.

   8.   Tell about a current event related to your topic.

   9.   Ask questions about your topic and explain why the
        questions are important.

   10. Begin with a startling quotation from one of your
        sources.

     When you have three introductions, ask other people to

read them and to discuss with you which of the three is best

for your paper.   Ask others for suggestions about ways you

might improve the introduction you like best.

Instructor´s OK: Completion date:_____

28

STEP 11: ORGANIZING AN OUTLINE   Due date:____

The first step in organizing an outline is to take your note cards off the photocopies and then group the cards according to slug lines.

Figure out in what order each group of cards will appear in your paper. It helps to reread your introduction and thesis statement and to switch the piles around until you come to an arrangement that pleases you.

Next, you have to decide how you want to order the cards in each pile. Reading the subheadings on the note cards will help you do this. You might also ask yourself: "What idea leads into what other idea?" Sequence your cards in the order you think will work for your paper.

On a sheet of paper, begin writing your outline. The slug for your first pile of cards will become "I" in your outline. Your subheadings will become "A," "B," etc. The second pile will become "II," and the subheads will be divisions of that section. Continue until all piles are accounted for.

Example:

    I. First slug

        A. First slug subheading
        B. Second slug subheading
        C. Third slug subheading

    II. Second slug

        A. First slug subheading
        B. Second slug subheading

If some of your note cards seem off the mark or repetitious, put them in a separate pile. Bind them with a rubber band and label the pile "unused note cards."

It is important for you to remember that at this stage the outline is temporary and will probably change as you write your draft. Consider this a tentative map that will help you to get started on your paper.

Instructor's OK: Completion date:_____

STEP 12A: WRITING THE FIRST DRAFT/DOCUMENTATION

Due date:____

You will need lined paper and a pen for this step. WRITE ON EVERY OTHER LINE THROUGHOUT THIS DRAFT AND WRITE ON ONLY ONE SIDE OF EACH SHEET.

Read over the introduction and thesis statement you've chosen for your paper, and unwrap your first pile of cards.

Imagining that each pile of cards represents a mini-paper in itself sometimes helps. Your own words will lead the reader to your first note card. Starting at the top of a new sheet of paper, introduce this section of your paper in your own words before you begin using your note cards.

Write the information from the first card on your draft, either copying it exactly or rephrasing it. At the end of this information, you must tell where it came from by putting parentheses around the author's last name (the title of the article if no author is given or if you have more than one article by the same author) and the exact page number(s) on which the information appears. This must be done whether you have quoted directly, paraphrased or summarized the information. ANY INFORMATION BORROWED FROM SOMEONE ELSE MUST BE DOCUMENTED.

When you have finished using the first card, turn it over and move on to the second.

As you move from card to card, try to connect the

information with words or sentences of your own. It helps to think of your own words as a frame for the note card information. Continue in this way until your first pile is finished.

The second pile of cards represents another main section of your paper. Begin writing this (and every) new section on a new sheet of paper. You will need to introduce the reader to this section as you did the first. Repeat the procedure, again imagining that this is the second mini-paper of your whole research paper.

Continue in this way until you have used all the note cards appropriate for your paper. Feel free to make adjustments as you write. You may find that some cards are repetitious or irrelevant. Set these cards aside.

When you have finished, take all the note cards you have used and make sure they are arranged in the order they appear in your paper. Put a rubber band around them and mark them "Used." Take the cards you haven´t used, put a rubber band around them, and mark them "Unused."

STEP 12B: TRANSITIONS

When you start to write your paper, you will already have a fairly good picture in your mind of how all the information you have on your cards is related and where you want to go with it. However, if you just plunk one note card after another into your paper without letting your reader know how the many bits of information are related to each other and how you have reacted to this information, your reader may finish reading your paper without ever being able to follow your line of thought or understand your picture of the topic. You need to take your reader by the hand and show her where you´re going and how you´re getting there. You can do this by using transitions--words, phrases, sentences and even paragraphs--which provide connections and guide your reader through each step you take in the development of your topic.

Here are some transitions you might find useful.

WORDS AND PHRASES:

   to indicate time: soon, immediately afterward, later,

   meanwhile, after a while, at last, since, until,

   while, lately

   to indicate place: nearby, here, beyond, opposite to

   to indicate result: as a result, therefore, thus,

   consequently, hence, then, therefore, accordingly

   to indicate comparison: likewise, similarly, in such

   a manner, also, as

   to indicate contrast: however, nevertheless, still,

   but, yet, on the other hand, after all, otherwise,

   although, yet

   to indicate addition: again, also, finally,

   further, in addition, moreover, last, first, second,

   third, . . ., too

   to indicate summarizing: as I have indicated,

in conclusion, to summarize

to indicate concession or partial aggreement:
naturally, of course, I admit, at the same time,
after all

to provide an "echo" from the preceding paragraph or
sentence. This may be done by repeating a key
phrase or word or a pronoun which refers back to
such a word or idea. You could also use a synonym
for a word or words in the preceding sentence. (See
Workbook page 48, where the word "homeless" serves
as a transition from the first paragraph to the
second. The sentence begins "Thinking about the way
the homeless live. . . .")

SENTENCES

You can develop a sentence to form a bridge between
paragraphs or major divisions in your paper. (See Workbook
page 51: "Just as there are many different kinds. . . .")

PARAGRAPHS

Entire paragraphs can be used as transitions. These are
especially helpful as you move from one main heading to
another or as you begin a new section of your paper. You
might use a transitional paragraph to ask a question whose
answer can launch the next section of your paper. In
addition, a transitional paragraph can be used to summarize
preceding information or to develop your own position about
the topic. (See Workbook page 54: "I agree. . . .")

STEP 12C: CONCLUSIONS

The best way to write your conclusion is similar to the way you wrote your introduction--write two or three possible endings and decide which one is best. Believe it or not, there is no specific time for writing a good ending. Maybe a brainstorm about your ending will occur to you in the research stage of your paper, or while you are writing the body of the paper. Keep your A-1 ideas jotted down in one place, and review all the material that has not found its way into your paper up to this point; you may find something there that you can use as a kernel for the ending. Write an ending as soon as you have finished writing the paper, while your pen is still smoking. Then, if you have time, put the paper away for a few days, take it out, reread it and write another ending. Your conclusion may end up being one of the above or a combination of two or more of them.

In either case, conclusions for a paper of any length have two parts: a BRIEF summary of the main points of the paper and a "clincher." The summary will help your reader recall the highlights of your research and the validity of your points as s/he is about to leave you. This part is easy to do: reread your introduction and thesis a few times, then think about a different and probably shorter way to restate it.

The second part of the conclusion is the place where you

can really let your creativity go wild. You can think of this part of your paper as the clincher--a kind of strong emotional statement at the end of your discussion or argument which will leave your reader thinking hard about your topic. Make it personal--ask yourself, "So what? What does this mean to me?" The conclusion is the place to let your own voice and emotions be heard.

You can also step back even further from your topic by attempting to show how it has meaning and impact in a broader context. Examine the conclusion of the sample research paper on pages 58-59 ("Every human being has the right . . ."), and you will see both these strategies at work. The writer makes an emotional statement about the topic, then shifts it to a larger context by reintroducing the Statue of Liberty and the values American stands for.

STEP 13:   REVISION OF ROUGH DRAFT   Due date:____

     After you have finished writing your rough draft, put it
aside for a day or two. Then read it again and share it with
a reviewer.   Letting the draft "cool off" makes it easier
for you to read it objectively. Plan to read through your
rough draft several times, at least once aloud. As you and
your reviewer read the draft, answer the questions on the
next page, and make changes where you feel they are
necessary.

     When you have completed the peer review sheet, you will
need to hand in to your instructor:

     1. your final revision

     2. used note cards (bound with a rubber band) arranged
         in the order in which they appear in the paper

     3. unused note cards (bound with a rubber band)

     4. used bib cards

     5. used photocopies

Instructor´s OK: Completion date:_____

Question:	Reviewer´s Answer	My answer
1. Does everything I´ve said in the paper connect clearly with my thesis?		
2. Do I present the ideas in my paper in a logical order?		
3. Is my thesis thoroughly developed?		
4. Does the order of ideas in my paper match my outline?		
5. Do I make the order of my paper easy for my reader to follow by using transitions?		
6. Have I used my own words to frame materials I have quoted, paraphrased, or summarized from my note cards?		
7. Have I documented all the note card information I have borrowed from my sources?		
8. Is the form of my documentation correct?		
9. Is each sentence in my paper clear and easy to understand?		
10. Is my conclusion climactic and appropriate?		

STEP 14: WRITING THE BIBLIOGRAPHY   Due date:_____

Gather the bib cards for the sources you used in your
paper.   Arrange them in alphabetical order according to the
last name of the author. If no author is given, alphabetize
according to the first word of the title (discounting the
words "a," "an" and "the"). If two articles are written by
the same author, alphabetize according to the first word of
the article.   Instead of repeating the author´s name in the
subsequent entry, simply type three hyphens followed by a
period. (See the bibliography on Workbook page 60.)

Write the word BIBLIOGRAPHY at the center of a sheet of
lined paper about one inch from the top. Skip one line and,
beginning at the left margin, copy the information from the
first card. If this information requires more than one line,
skip a line, and indent following lines five spaces.
Doublespace throughout the bibliography.

Place your bibliography at the end of your rough draft.

Here are some forms you may need in your bibliography.

<u>Magazine entry</u>:

Alter, Jonathan. "Homeless in America." <u>Newsweek</u>

    2 January 1984: 20-23+.

NewsBank entry:

Goldman, Henry. "A Look at Life in the Streets: Court Told
    How the Homeless Live." Philadelphia (Pennsylvania)
    Inquirer 20 April 1985. NewsBank, Welfare, 1985,
    fiche 16, grid E8.

More than one author:

Hopper, Kim, and Ellen Baxter. "Letters." Scientific
    American October 1984: 8.

SIRS entry:

Lyons, Richard D. "How Release of Mental Patients Began."
    New York Times 30 October 1984. SIRS, Mental
    Health, volume 3, article 16.

Scholarly journal entry:

Stern, M. J. "The Emergence of the Homeless As a Public
    Problem." Social Service Review 58 (1984): 291-301.

Government publication:

U. S. Senate Committee on Appropriations. Street People.
    Washington, D. C.: Government Printing Office, 1983.

Newspaper entry:

Waggoner, Walter H. "Some Givers Believe the City's
    Neediest are Its Street People." New York Times 16
    December 1983: B20, col. 1.

    If you need a bib form that is not presented here, ask
your instructor or refer to the latest edition of MLA
Handbook for Writers of Research Papers.

Instructor's OK: Completion date:____

STEP 15: TYPING THE PAPER

GENERAL RULES

Use white typing paper, 8 1/2" by 11".

Doublespace throughout your paper.

Leave a one-inch margin all around.

Indent five spaces for paragraphs.

Space twice after a period, colon and question mark;
space once after a comma and semi-colon.

TITLE PAGE

Center your title about halfway down the page,
capitalizing the first and all key words. Do not
underline the title. Do not use quotation marks
unless you are using a direct quote.

Move down two lines and center the word "by."

Move down two lines and center your name.

Move down two lines and center the date.

OUTLINE PAGE

Type the word "Thesis" followed by a colon. Then type
your thesis statement.

Type your outline, beginning with "I." Indent
subheadings A, B, C, etc. (It is incorrect to have
only one division of a heading. If you have an A,
you must have a B. If you have a 1, you must have
a 2.)

BODY

Begin typing one inch from the top of your sheet. Enclose direct quotes in quotation marks. Put beginning quotation marks immediately before the first word of the quote; put the closing set immediately after the last word. Then type parentheses for documentation with the closing punctuation for the sentence following the closing parenthesis.

If you have a direct quote that is longer than three typewritten lines, it must be set off from the body of your paper. Indent all lines of the quote ten spaces from the left margin. Do not enclose the quote in quotation marks. Follow the closing punctuation with documentation in parentheses. When you have finished, continue with your text. (See pages 51 and 54 of the Workbook.)

Each page number is typed in the upper right hand corner, beginning with the first page of the text.

BIBLIOGRAPHY

Type BIBLIOGRAPHY or WORKS CITED about one inch from the top of the page. Skip a line and begin typing your first entry at the left margin. Indent all other lines of that entry five spaces. Begin each new entry at the left margin. Doublespace throughout the bibliography.

STEP 16:   COMPLETION OF RESEARCH PAPER   Due date:_____
            AND EVALUATION

When you have completed the typing of your paper, read it slowly aloud to catch any typing errors. Correct these errors in ink on the typed copy.

After your instructor has graded your research paper and returned it to you, read through the paper carefully and note your instructor's comments. Then write a final process note on the back of this sheet. Include what you have learned from the research paper process and how you feel about your paper and your grade.

CONGRATULATIONS!

Instructor's OK: Completion date:_____

Process notes

THE RAINBOW: DEMONSTRATION MODEL

"Send These, the Homeless Tempest-tossed, to Me"

(Inscription on the Statue of Liberty)

by

Susan R. Ide

July 17, 1985

Thesis: Because of how they live, who they are, and why they are homeless, we are all morally responsible for helping our nation's homeless through increased federal funding for effective programs.

OUTLINE

I.   Lifestyle of the Homeless

    A.   Food

    B.   Daily activities

    C.   Sleeping

    D.   Health

    E.   Relationships

II. Number of homeless

III. Profile of homeless

    A.   Alcoholism

    B.   Gender

    C.   Age

    D.   Race

    E.   Education

    F.   Homeless families

    G.   Mental illness

IV. Causes of homelessness

    A.   Deinstitutionalization

        1.   Possible because of psychoactive drugs

        2.   Desirable to humanitarians

        3.   Mandated by law

B.   Unemployment

   C.   Cutbacks in government benefits

   D.   Urban renewal

   E.   Tolerance of homelessness

V. Solutions

   A.   Negative

   B.   Positive

        1.   Awareness of problem

        2.   Funding

        3.   Program and policy implementation

             a.   Private organizations

             b.   Federal government

             c.   States

When I was a child, they were called bums--those men slumped on New York City street curbs or floundering along on sidewalks and poking well-dressed people's elbows to beg for money. They terrified me and turned my stomach, but they also fascinated me. Their eyes were red-rimmed and bleary in purply faces with blue veins and stubbly gray whiskers. They wore baggy trousers and shapeless, filthy topcoats even in summer. I assumed they were all drunks. I remember occasionally seeing women, too, in get-ups like circus clowns, fumbling through sidewalk garbage containers in New York City. They aroused my curiosity rather than frightened me. Now people call them "bag ladies," a term which suggests that they are comical. During the past few years, the media have made me aware that today there are many more men and women literally living on city streets than there were when I was a child. Today reporters call them "the homeless," a term that expresses much more sympathy and respect for them than "bum" or "bag lady." From now on I will think of them with compassion as "the homeless" because my research has convinced me that the horrible way they live is not their choice and seldom their fault. Their problems are the responsiblity of all of us. They need and deserve our help--my help.

Thinking about the way the homeless live makes me cringe because they live like stray cats and dogs. For food they typically eat out of restaurant dumpsters or go to soup kitchens where they may have to wait in long lines (Alter, "Homeless in America" 21). Some of them spend their days trying to earn a little money by collecting returnable bottles, selling their blood, or volunteering to be guinea pigs in experiments (Bassuk 44). They sleep just about anywhere they can from dumpsters to mortuaries (Andersen 14). One man "was living in a tomb he had hollowed out" in a cemetery (Bassuk 43). Even many of the shelters provided by government or private charity are awful. A public shelter in New York City "regularly features an inch of water on a floor where people sleep and two-hour waits for showers" (Alter, "H. in A." 23).

It is not surprising that many of the homeless are in poor physical condition. A Boston study showed 45% had serious diseases (Bassuk 43). Among the health problems of the homeless are cancer, heart disease, tuberculosis, Salmonella, dysentery, frost bite and drug withdrawal (Bassuk 43; Andersen 14; Fustero 59). In January 1984 in New York City, "an average of one homeless person a day . . . [was] found dead in the streets" (Alter, "H. in A." 22). The homeless tend to live and die alone. In the Boston study 74% said "they had no family relationships" and 73% said "they had no friends, even within the shelter community" (Bassuk 43).

The number of homeless is difficult to estimate. The

figure most often cited in the sources I read was over 2 million, although the Federal Department of Housing and Urban Development (HUD) says there are only 250,000 to 350,000 (Bassuk 40). According to psychiatrist Ellen Bassuk, "Whatever the number is, everyone agrees it is growing" (40). Almost all the homeless live in cities. For example, Seattle and Detroit reported a 50% increase in demand for shelter from 1981 to 1983 (Easterbrook 10; Alter, "H. in A." 20). About 50,000 homeless are in New York City, 20,000 in Chicago, and 2,767 in Boston (Easterbrook 10; Stanley 28). Homelessness is a national problem because there are homeless people in all parts of the United States.

Who are these homeless people? Are they mostly old drunks, as I supposed? Ellen Bassuk and her colleagues found that only 29% of the homeless in the Boston shelter they studied were chronic alcoholics (43). Although the great majority of the homeless are men, the number of women seems to be increasing (Bassuk 42). The average homeless person is about 35 years old (Andersen 14), much younger than I would have thought. In New York City 20,000 of the homeless are under 21 (Alter "H. in A." 22). Although 80% of the homeless in New York City are black (Stanley 28), homelessness in general does not seem to involve one race more than another. In Phoenix the homeless include Mexicans and American Indians (Fustero 59-60). Many of the homeless are illiterate, but, surprisingly, they seem to include the same percentage of

college graduates as the general population (Andersen 14).
Though most of the homeless are solitary individuals, growing
numbers are members of homeless families.

> The U. S. Department of Housing and Urban
> Development's national shelter survey found
> that 21% of the shelter population today is
> made up of family members. In such places
> as New York City the population is even higher:
> homeless family members in emergency
> accommodations currently outnumber the single
> homeless in shelters by a ratio of 1.7 to one.
> (Hopper and Baxter 8)

Many, perhaps even most, of the homeless are mentally
ill. In her Boston study, Ellen Bassuk determined that 90%
of those she examined were mentally ill. She includes
chronic alcoholics (29%) and people with severe personality
disorders (21%) in this figure, but asserts that 40% of those
she studied are psychotic, mostly schizophrenics (Bassuk
42-43). Probably using a narrower definition of mental
illness, the New York State Office of Mental Health also
estimated in 1983 that 30% to 50% of the homeless were
mentally ill (Stanley 28).

Just as there are many different kinds of street people,
so there are many reasons for their homelessness. The four
major causes result from nationwide social trends sometimes
reinforced by law. These major causes are the

deinstitutionalization of mental patients, a high
unemployment rate, cutbacks in federal welfare programs, and
a growing shortage of low-income housing.

Deinstitutionalization began in the 1950s when the use
of "psychoactive drugs" as therapy for the mentally ill made
it possible for them to get treatment outside of institutions
(Bassuk 41). Mainstreaming the mentally ill has seemed to
the public, the Congress and the courts a humanitarian change
that would provide a better life for the mentally ill than an
institution would. In 1971 the Alabama law suit of Wyatt vs.
Stickney made deinstitutionalization of the mentally ill law
and guaranteed them "the right to treatment in the least
restrictive setting" (Fustero 58). Furthermore, courts have
ruled that only the mentally ill who are "dangerous to
themselves or to others may be committed involuntarily"
(Bassuk 42). The result of all this is that there are many
mentally ill people on the streets who in the past would have
been in institutions (Bassuk 42). For example, in 1955 there
were 550,000 people in state institutions for the mentally
ill, compared with 125,000 today (Fustero 58). Many
deinstitutionalized people are homeless because no one wants
to be bothered with them and/or because they are too confused
to take advantage of services available to them. Because
"many are chronically, permanently ill and will never be able
to live independently" (Bassuk 44), they need more help than
just the busfare to another city, which is all they are

sometimes given upon discharge from an institution (Fustero 58). They cannot be expected to support themselves because most of them cannot possibly hold a full-time job.

For the homeless who could hold a job, often there are no jobs. In 1982 our national unemployment rate was 10.7% (Bassuk 41). Among young black men in New York City, the current rate is 40 to 50% (Fustero 59), and among American Indians on reservations it is also close to 50% (Fustero 60). Many of the homeless are recent high school graduates who have no job skills. The "menial jobs" most homeless men have been able to find (Alter, "H. in A." 22) have either not lasted or have not provided a living wage.

Cutbacks in federal benefits have blown the roof off some homeless people. Between March 1981 and April 1984, about 150,000 to 200,000 people lost benefits because of the Reagan Administration´s "crackdown on ineligibility" for Social Security Disability payments (Bassuk 41). After losing financial aid, many could no longer afford to pay rent, even for low-rent housing. In the fall of 1982, 11.7% of 681 new arrivals in New York City shelters had been evicted (Easterbrook 16). In December 1983, one third of the homeless families in New York City had lost their homes because they couldn´t pay the rent (Andersen 15).

Sometimes poor people lose their homes because of urban renewal. Many low-rental buildings, especially those with single-room-occupancy (SRO), have been condemned and razed or

renovated for urban renewal projects. Between 1970 and 1980
about one million SROs were eliminated nationwide (Alter, "H.
in A." 23). Although some of these lost accommodations have
evidently been replaced by new low-income housing, "fewer
than half of the 6 million low-income units Lyndon Johnson
believed were needed in 1968 ever got built" (Alter, "H. in
A." 22). Couple this lack of low-income housing with the
fact that in the 1970s average rent increased "twice as fast
as income" (Alter, "H. in A." 22), and it's easy to see how
many people have been shoved into the streets.

Whatever the cause, some people have suggested that we
continue to have homelessness in this country because we
accept it.

> In a round-table discussion sponsored by ADMAHA
> [the Alcohol, Drug Abuse and Mental Health
> Administration] last spring, professionals who
> work with the homeless cited this tolerance
> as an important reason that homelessness has
> never been resolved or effectively dealt with.
> (Fustero 60)

I agree that we should stop tolerating homelessness, but
not by punishing the homeless, as some cities have done. In
Phoenix after 1982, a person caught going through garbage got
the same treatment and penalty as a thief. Zoning laws were
passed and buildings were condemned to get rid of services
for the homeless (Fustero 60). In 1983 Phoenix provided no

overnight beds for the homeless, but there were still 3,000
homeless in the city (Easterbrook 10). Last winter in
Greenwich Village "odd-shaped metal boxes and barbed wire
were placed across hot-air exhaust grates to keep homeless
people from sleeping in the neighborhood" (Leo 68). Such
measures are inhumane. Furthermore, even if they eliminate
or diminish homelessness in some places, they do not solve
the problem nationally because homeless people are simply
forced to move from an intolerant city to a more tolerant
one.

We should stop tolerating homelessness by eliminating
its causes and by providing adequate and effective
alternatives for street people. The first step toward a
solution to the problem of homelessness is national awareness
of the problem and an understanding that most of the homeless
are victims rather than voluntary vagrants. The media have
helped to accomplish this first step. The homeless
themselves have cooperated in group actions to force
awareness on government and the public. The Coalition for
the Homeless with its attorney Robert M. Hayes won a lawsuit
to make New York City government set up shelters for the
homeless with places to eat and "lockers, toilets and
showers" (Fustero 61). In 1984 the Community for Creative
Non-Violence and many homeless people protested Reagan´s cuts
in aid programs by staging a tent-in at Lafayette Park in
front of the White House (Fustero 61). The federal

government is aware of the problem.   A hearing on

homelessness was held in December 1982 by a House

subcommittee--the first such congressional hearing since 1933

during the Depression (Easterbrook 16).

A second step toward solving the problem of homelessness

is funding, which currently comes from volunteer groups and

all levels of government.   The total expenditure on the

homeless in 1983 by both governments and charity in the

United States was about $500 million (Andersen 14).   But even

this much money is not enough.   If there are 2 million

homeless people, $250 per person per year is clearly

inadequate.   The only fair way for all of us to meet our

financial responsibility to the homeless is through increased

federal spending of tax dollars.

Although step two, funding, should be the responsibility

of the federal government, private organizations should be

responsible for step three: providing food, shelter and

other services for the homeless.   The reason is that

government projects can cost up to ten times what private

projects cost.   In San Francisco, for example, private

construction of housing for the poor cost only $8,000 per

unit, compared to $80,000 per unit for HUD-directed

construction of housing for the poor in the same city.

Government costs are so high because of strict specifications

tied to expenditure of federal money.   Even if private

organizations use federal money to aid the homeless, some

federal regulations will have to be modified (Easterbrook 20).

True, the federal government could do more to help the homeless than supply money and relax some regulations about how the money is spent. The 170,000 "abandoned dwellings" that HUD owns throughout the country could become homes for the homeless (Easterbrook 24). Writer Gregg Easterbrook suggests, "Why not employ a federal work corps to renovate empty buildings for use as housing? The program would create meaningful jobs and make decent again communities where most of the unemployed live" (24). This sounds like an excellent idea, except that a government-run project would probably be too expensive. Easterbrook acknowledges other problems: Republicans in Congress are unlikely to vote for such an idea because they are philosophically opposed to federal social programs; Democrats, who are usually union-supported, are unlikely to vote for a program that would use non-union labor (Easterbrook 24). There might be hope for a program like Easterbrook's if both Republican and Democratic voters flooded their Congressmen's offices with calls and letters demanding such a program.

Furthermore, the federal government can help the large group of mentally ill homeless by passing the McKinney bill. Current law requires that the mentally ill be treated in "the least restrictive setting." The McKinney bill would change

the wording to "optimum therapeutic settings" (Fustero 61).
Ironically, life in an institution seems better than life on
the streets. The McKinney bill would also put pressure on
states to provide proper treatment for the mentally ill or
else forfeit federal funds (Fustero 61).

Massachusetts has demonstrated some ways that state
governments can help the homeless. In the fall of 1983
Massachusetts changed state law to allow people without
permanent addresses to receive welfare benefits (Andersen
15). As of January 1984, Massachusetts tenants in buildings
to be razed or renovated must have up to four years´ notice
before being evicted. Massachusetts also established a
24-hour hot-line for homeless referrals and assigned more
caseworkers to serve the homeless (Alter "F.B." 26).

Every human being has the right to food and shelter.
All of us--through our city, state, and federal governments
and through our charitable organizations--must take
responsibility for solving the problem of homelessness. Jobs
must be available to those who are capable of living
independently. For those who are permanently disabled by
mental illness or other problems, we must provide permanent
residences that include food, services and whatever therapy
is needed. We must devise programs that will put the
homeless in touch with the services they need, and when
necessary, we must teach them skills they need to lead more
normal lives.

The Statue of Liberty invites the world´s homeless to
our shores. In a country that prides itself on its
humanitarianism and threatens to boycott other countries that
deny their citizens´ civil rights, failure to solve the
problem of our homeless is hypocritical and immoral.

Bibliography

Alter, Jonathan, et. al. "Fighting Back." <u>Newsweek</u>
     2 January 1984: 26.

---. "Homeless in America." <u>Newsweek</u> 2 January
     1984: 20-23+.

Andersen, Kurt. "Left Out in the Cold." <u>Time</u> 19
     December 1983: 14-15.

Bassuk, Ellen L. "The Homelessness Problem." <u>Scientific
     American</u> July 1984: 40-45.

Easterbrook, Gregg. "Examining a Media Myth." <u>The
     Atlantic</u> October 1983: 10+.

Fustero, Steven. "Home on the Street." <u>Psychology
     Today</u> February 1984: 56-63.

Hopper, Kim, and Ellen Baxter. "Letters." <u>Scientific
     American</u> October 1984: 8.

Leo, John. "Harassing the Homeless." <u>Time</u>
     11 March 1985: 68.

Stanley, Kay O. "Homeless Data Debate." <u>Black
     Enterprise</u> November 1984: 28.